WEST VIRGINIA

W9-BNM-662

WEST VIRGINIA

HELLO
U.S.A.

by Domenica Di Piazza

Lerner Publications Company

You'll find this picture of a monarch butterfly's wing at the beginning of each chapter in this book. The monarch was chosen as West Virginia's state butterfly in 1995. Monarch butterflies travel south from West Virginia to Mexico for the winter, where they gather in huge groups. In May the monarchs return to West Virginia to lay eggs, which become full-grown adults by August.

Cover (left): Glade Creek grist mill, Babcock State Park. Cover (right): White-water rafters on New River. Pages 2–3: Charleston on the Kanawha River. Page 3: Old town in Harpers Ferry National Historical Park.

This book is available in two editions:
Library binding by Lerner Publications Company, a division of Lerner Publishing Group
Soft cover by First Avenue Editions, an imprint of Lerner Publishing Group
241 First Avenue North
Minneapolis, MN 55401 U.S.A.

Website address: www.lernerbooks.com

Library of Congress Cataloging-in-Publication Data

Di Piazza, Domenica.
    West Virginia / by Domenica Di Piazza. (Rev. and expanded 2nd ed.)
        p.   cm. — (Hello U.S.A.)
    Includes index.
    ISBN: 0–8225–4068–1 (lib. bdg. : alk paper)
    ISBN: 0–8225–4141–6 (pbk. : alk. paper)
    1. West Virginia—Juvenile literature.   [1. West Virginia.]   I. Title.
    II. Series.
    F241 .D52 2002
    975.4—dc21
                                                                                      2001002957

Manufactured in the United States of America
1 2 3 4 5 6 – JR – 07 06 05 04 03 02

CONTENTS

The forests of the Alleghenies *(above)* are home to oak trees, one of West Virginia's most common trees. An early frost *(inset)* covers the deep red leaves of an oak.

The Mountain State

I f you're looking for flat land in West Virginia, chances are you won't have much luck. Mountains and steep hills rise from one end of the state to the other. For this reason, West Virginia is known as the Mountain State, and residents call themselves Mountaineers.

West Virginia's rugged landscape is part of a large mountain system called the Appalachians. Millions of years ago, the area that later became West Virginia was almost flat. But over time, huge layers of rock folded and lifted upward to form the Appalachian Mountains. Rain, wind, and rushing rivers carved out deep valleys.

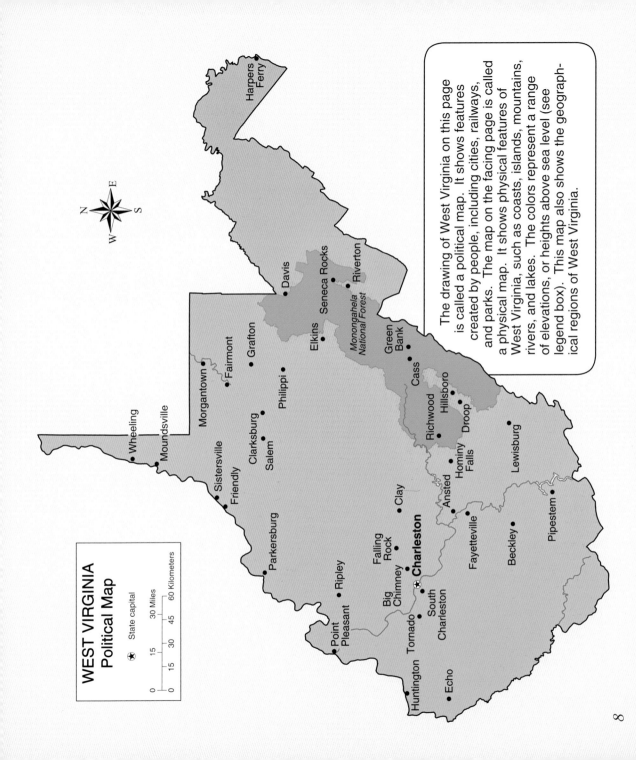

WEST VIRGINIA
Political Map

★ State capital

0   15   30 Miles
0 15 30 45 60 Kilometers

The drawing of West Virginia on this page is called a political map. It shows features created by people, including cities, railways, and parks. The map on the facing page is called a physical map. It shows physical features of West Virginia, such as coasts, islands, mountains, rivers, and lakes. The colors represent a range of elevations, or heights above sea level (see legend box). This map also shows the geographical regions of West Virginia.

Harpers Ferry

Davis

Seneca Rocks

Riverton

Grafton

Fairmont

Morgantown

Elkins

Monongahela National Forest

Green Bank

Cass

Philippi

Wheeling

Moundsville

Clarksburg

Salem

Richwood

Hillsboro

Droop

Hominy Falls

Lewisburg

Sistersville

Friendly

Clay

Ansted

Parkersburg

Falling Rock

Charleston

Fayetteville

Beckley

Pipestem

Ripley

Big Chimney

South Charleston

Point Pleasant

Huntington

Tornado

Echo

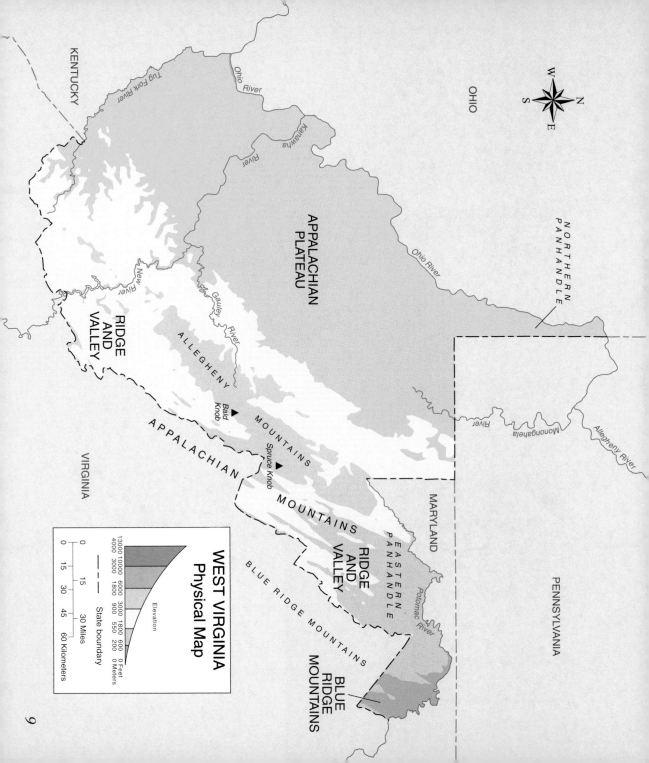

KENTUCKY

OHIO

Tug Fork River

Ohio River

Ohio River

Kanawha River

N
W — E
S

NORTHERN
PANHANDLE

APPALACHIAN
PLATEAU

Gauley River

New River

RIDGE
AND
VALLEY

A L L E G H E N Y

M O U N T A I N S

Bald
Knob ▲

Spruce Knob ▲

VIRGINIA

A P P A L A C H I A N

M O U N T A I N S

Monongahela River

Allegheny River

MARYLAND

RIDGE
AND
VALLEY

E A S T E R N
P A N H A N D L E

Potomac River

PENNSYLVANIA

B L U E R I D G E M O U N T A I N S

BLUE
RIDGE
MOUNTAINS

WEST VIRGINIA
Physical Map

Elevation	
Feet	Meters
13000	4000
10000	3000
6000	1800
3000	900
1800	550
600	200
0	0

— — — State boundary

0   15   30   45   60 Kilometers
0   15   30 Miles

The Blue Ridge Mountains stretch across the Eastern Panhandle.

West Virginia is easy to identify on a map because it is the only state in the country with two panhandles. They are known as the Eastern Panhandle and the Northern Panhandle. These areas of land are shaped something like the handles on frying pans. Mountaineers sometimes joke that their state is a great place, considering the shape it's in.

A Mid-Atlantic state, West Virginia shares its borders with five other states. Across the Ohio River, to the west, lies Ohio. To the southwest, across the Tug Fork River, is Kentucky. Mountain peaks separate West Virginia from Virginia in the east. Maryland lies to the northeast, and Pennsylvania borders the northwest.

West Virginia has three regions—the Blue Ridge Mountains, the Ridge and Valley, and the Appalachian Plateau. These regions are part of the Appalachian system, which covers the entire state.

The Blue Ridge Mountains rise in the northeastern corner of West Virginia. When seen from far away, the forested slopes of this range appear blue—the color for which the mountains are named. Farmers raise fruit trees in the region's river valleys.

Farms dot the hills of the Allegheny Mountains, which are part of the larger Appalachian system.

The Ridge and Valley runs the length of West Virginia's eastern border. Extending over much of the region are the Allegheny Mountains, where the state's highest peak—Spruce Knob—rises. Rivers wind through narrow valleys that separate these tree-covered ridges.

The Appalachian Plateau covers the rest of West Virginia. Most of the state's biggest cities are located in the river valleys of the **plateau**, an area of high land. Rich deposits of minerals such as coal, petroleum, natural gas, and salt lie underground in this region.

Cities like Charleston (*below*) have sprung up in West Virginia's river valleys.

For more than 100 years, West Virginians have relied on rivers for shipping coal and other minerals to market. The Mountaineers built cities near these busy water highways. Huntington and Wheeling, two of the state's largest cities, grew along the banks of the Ohio River. Charleston, the state capital, lies along the Kanawha River. Other important waterways in the state include the Monongahela, the Potomac, and the New River.

Snow blankets a West Virginia forest.

West Virginia receives about 50 inches of **precipitation** (rain, sleet, hail, and snow) every year. Most of the snow falls in the mountains, where up to 100 inches may blanket the highest peaks in winter. Less than 20 inches of snow falls in the southwest.

Winters in West Virginia are coldest high up in the mountains. Midwinter temperatures on the slopes average about 22° F. Temperatures in the valleys stay several degrees warmer. In summer, people

Forests are both common and important in West Virginia. They are home to many of the state's animals, and they add to the beauty of the state.

living high in the mountains enjoy cooler weather than residents of cities such as Charleston. The average summer temperature in this river town is about 87° F.

Anglers find plenty of bass, trout, and walleye in West Virginia's rivers and streams. Foxes, opossums, and raccoons make their homes in the state's forests. Bears, deer, and beavers outnumber people in some areas.

One of the first flowers to bloom every spring in West Virginia is the hepatica (*above*). In a West Virginia forest, a fawn takes a nap (*left*).

Bears are native to
West Virginia's forests.

West Virginia's forests stretch across most of the state. Evergreen trees, such as white pine, red spruce, and hemlock, grow on mountainsides and in river valleys. Hardwoods include maple, cherry, oak, and tulip trees. Dogwood, redbud, hawthorn, and other flowering trees open their buds each spring in the state's river valleys.

Early summer is a great time to see the colorful blossoms of West Virginia's state flower, the rhododendron. Asters and black-eyed Susans bloom into the fall. And Mountaineers know it's spring again when dainty hepatica flowers begin to bud.

From Hunting to Mining

The first people in North America were hunters. Scientists believe that these people came from Asia at least 15,000 years ago by walking across a land bridge that once connected these two continents. Over thousands of years, descendants of the early hunters made their way to the area that became West Virginia.

Traveling in small groups, the hunters moved from place to place and used spears to kill mammoths and other large prey. These huge animals became extinct around 8000 B.C. The people then survived by fishing, hunting smaller game such as deer, and gathering nuts and berries.

Descendants of the hunters and gatherers began building permanent villages along the Ohio River around 1000 B.C. Villagers raised pumpkins and sunflowers for food and tobacco to smoke during special ceremonies. Round homes built from poles, mud, and bark provided shelter for families.

Over 10,000 years ago, mammoths roamed the area that later became West Virginia. By studying their bones, scientists have learned that some mammoths stood more than 14 feet tall and had tusks 13 feet long.

The Grave Creek Mound near Moundsville, West Virginia, contains about 60,000 tons of dirt. It is the largest mound of its kind in the United States.

Chiefs and priests lived on top of huge earthen mounds. When they died, these leaders were buried in log tombs covered with many piles of dirt. Because they constructed so many giant earthworks, these people came to be known as mound builders.

Most of the mounds in what later became West Virginia were built along the Ohio and Kanawha Rivers, but other mounds were scattered across the region. By about A.D. 1500, the mound builders had abandoned their villages. No one knows exactly what happened, but experts think that warfare, disease, or lack of rain may have forced the mound builders to leave their homes.

European fur traders arrived in the West Virginia area in the 1600s.

At about the same time, far across the Atlantic Ocean, Great Britain and other European countries imagined North America to be a land of many riches. Hoping to gain some of this wealth, these countries began to set up **colonies**, or settlements, in America. In 1607 three boats carrying British settlers landed at the mouth of the James River in the Virginia Colony.

Recently founded by Great Britain, the colony stretched between modern-day Pennsylvania and South Carolina. The colony's western boundaries, however, had not been established.

Traders soon began to explore the Virginia Colony in search of valuable fur-bearing animals such as beavers. In 1671 an expedition led by Thomas Batts and Robert Fallam crossed the Alleghenies into eastern West Virginia. There, they claimed the New River Valley for Great Britain.

Farther west, French fur traders were exploring the Ohio River Valley. They hoped to expand their fur-trading business in North America. The French and the British met Native Americans, or Indians, from many different nations in West Virginia. These groups, possibly descended from the early mound builders, included the Cherokee, the Shawnee, the Delaware, the Mingo, and the Iroquois Indians.

Some Indians hunted game animals by trapping the prey in rings of fire.

Although the Indians did not make permanent homes in what would become West Virginia, they used the area as a hunting ground. Indians supplied the Europeans with furs and received kettles, beads, and hatchets in exchange. Traders transported the furs to European countries, where the pelts sold for high prices.

As the British expanded their fur trade west toward the Ohio River, German and Scotch-Irish farmers came to West Virginia. Over time these pioneers claimed more and more territory. Settlers and Native Americans disagreed about who had rights to the land, and fighting sometimes broke out.

Meanwhile, the British and the French were arguing over the Ohio River Valley. The British believed that Batts and Fallam had claimed the land in 1671. But the French believed that the valley belonged to France, since French adventurers had explored the region as well.

French settlers tried to keep control of the Ohio River Valley by burying lead plates inscribed with their claim to the land.

West Virginians developed many of their cities around forts, such as Fort Fincastle (later Fort Henry) near Wheeling. Settlers fled to the forts for protection during attacks and battles.

By 1754 the disagreement had led to the French and Indian War. Some of the bloodiest battles of this conflict were fought in West Virginia. The French encouraged their Indian allies to attack British pioneers in the area. As a result, few new settlers came to the region.

After winning the war in 1763, Great Britain gained control of almost all the land between the Atlantic Ocean and the Mississippi River. Five years later, the British signed **treaties**, or agreements, with the Cherokee and the Iroquois nations. In exchange for a payment, these Indian nations gave up their claim to most of their land in West Virginia. After this, thousands of settlers came to the region.

Lord Dunmore's War

After the French and Indian War, thousands of pioneers made their way to the area that became West Virginia. Many of these settlers built homes in the Ohio River Valley, on land that Indian nations had not given up. As a result, settlers and Indians often clashed violently.

In an attack in April 1774, settlers killed the family of a Mingo chief named Logan (above left). Logan, who had been friendly to white people for many years, felt betrayed and took up arms. He was joined by the Shawnee leader Cornstalk and his forces. Under Cornstalk, Indian troops battled the army of Lord Dunmore (above right), the governor of the Virginia Colony.

The conflict, known as Lord Dunmore's War, ended when Lord Dunmore defeated the Indians at the Battle of Point Pleasant that fall.

Logan, who had been asked to come to the peace negotiations, chose not to attend. Instead he sent a letter expressing his thoughts about the events that had led to the war. In the famous letter, Logan wrote that because his entire family had been murdered, "There runs not a drop of my blood in the veins of any living creature. This called upon me for revenge. I have sought it. . . . I rejoice at the beams of peace. . . . [But] who is there to mourn for Logan? Not one."

George Washington, a Virginian who had led British troops during the French and Indian War, owned land in West Virginia. But he was soon asked to lead troops in another war—the American War of Independence.

In this war, which started in 1775, British colonists in North America fought to win their independence from Great Britain. Many settlers from West Virginia fought in the colonial army. Others sewed clothing and grew crops to help feed colonial soldiers.

The American War of Independence lasted almost eight years. Many West Virginians joined the fight.

In 1789, following the American War of Independence, George Washington became the first president of a new country—the United States of America.

The colonists finally defeated the British in 1783 and formed a new country—the United States of America. Six years later, George Washington became the new nation's first president. Virginia, which included West Virginia, became one of the first states.

At the time, few people lived in western Virginia. But as settlers built new roads across the Allegheny Mountains, more people came to the region.

Many of the newcomers were farmers. Others were attracted by salt-mining jobs near Charleston in the Kanawha River Valley. Laborers found jobs mining coal to fuel the furnaces where salt was

produced. Workers crafted wooden barrels for shipping the salt to market. By 1815 salt furnaces in the Charleston area were manufacturing about 3,000 bushels of salt every day.

Agricultural industries were also booming. Blacksmiths fashioned plows and other farm equipment from iron bars made by the region's iron workers. Factories in growing cities such as Wheeling made clothing out of sheep's wool from the Northern Panhandle.

Miners digging for salt discovered oil in West Virginia. They threw the oil into nearby waterways because they had little use for it. At one time, the Kanawha River (*left*) became known as Old Greasy because it was so full of oil.

West Virginia's bumpy roads were so rough that carriage rides along them were known as "shake-guts."

From Wheeling, steamboats loaded with cattle, flour, glass, and wool headed to towns along the Ohio and Mississippi Rivers. After the Baltimore & Ohio Railroad laid tracks to Wheeling in 1852, trains began transporting goods to cities on the eastern side of the Appalachians.

At this time, railroads and trade were linking communities across the country. But many Americans were still divided over the issue of slavery. In Northern states, slavery was illegal. But many farmers in Virginia and other Southern states used slaves to work huge farms called **plantations**.

John Brown's Raid

John Brown spent much of his life working to end slavery. In the 1850s, he planned to set up a community of African Americans in the Appalachians in West Virginia. From there, Brown could lead attacks against slaveholders, actions he hoped would lead to a massive slave rebellion. To do this, Brown needed weapons and ammunition.

On October 16, 1859, Brown and a small army of supporters seized a warehouse in Harpers Ferry, West Virginia, where the U.S. government stored weapons. Word of the raid spread, and U.S. marines captured and arrested the group. Although Brown was tried for treason and hanged, his dream of ending slavery came true soon after his death.

The North pressured the South to end slavery, but Southern planters were determined to keep slaves. In early 1861 Southern states formed the Confederate States of America (the Confederacy), an independent country where slavery remained legal. Virginians were split over whether to join the new country. Most of the state's slaves worked on tobacco plantations east of the Alleghenies. To the west, the land was too mountainous for large farms. Most farmers did not own slaves.

The Civil War broke out between the North and the South in April 1861. Virginia soon voted to join the Confederacy. But most people in northwestern Virginia supported the North (the Union). In 1862 they approved a **constitution** (a set of basic written laws) for a new state to be called West Virginia. On June 20, 1863, the U.S. government admitted West Virginia as the 35th state.

Although most soldiers in West Virginia fought for the Union, at least 8,000 men joined the army of the Confederacy. Some families were bitterly split, with fathers and sons fighting on opposite sides.

In memory of John Brown, Union soldiers marching to battle sang, "John Brown's body lies a-moldering in the grave. His soul goes marching on."

In the early part of the war, Union troops defeated the Confederates in West Virginia and kept control of the state. But some Confederate soldiers fought back. They burned bridges and villages, destroyed homes, and stole salt, crops, and livestock. In 1865, after over four years of conflict, the Union won the war.

During the late 1800s, workers in West Virginia used picks and shovels to build railroad tracks.

Several new railroad companies built tracks across West Virginia after the Civil War. The tracks led into remote forests and opened up areas rich in coal and oil. Towns sprang up almost overnight along the tracks or wherever a new mine opened.

Mining and logging industries boomed in West Virginia in the late 1800s. By 1899 workers at nearly 1,000 sawmills across the state were producing lumber for wood products such as boats, houses, and railroad ties. Each year wells were pumping more than 10 million barrels of oil, and coal miners were digging up more than 18 million tons of coal.

As industries grew, so did West Virginia's population, which rose to almost 1 million people in 1900. Some of the new residents were Italian, Polish, Hungarian, Austrian, and Russian **immigrants**, who had come to the United States hoping for a better life. Many of these new-comers found jobs in West Virginia's coal mines.

By the end of the 1800s, railroads linked many of West Virginia's towns. They transported people and goods faster than carriages or steamships could.

During the early 1900s, more West Virginian coal miners died on the job than in any other coal-mining state.

Miners worked deep under the ground and faced many dangers on the job. Coal dust that collected in the mines caused a deadly disease called black lung. Poisonous gases built up in the mines. The gases sometimes caused explosions, which killed hundreds of miners.

In the early 1900s, many of West Virginia's coal miners joined a union (workers' organization) called the United Mine Workers of America (UMWA). The union organized strikes among its members, who refused to work unless their employers provided safer working conditions and better pay.

Most mining companies were angered by the strikes and forced new employees to sign papers agreeing not to join the union. The companies also hired guards to prevent union organizers from coming to talk to miners. The miners who did join the UMWA were sometimes beaten up by company guards or locked out of their homes, which were usually owned by the coal-mining companies.

Mary ("Mother") Jones, a famous union organizer, came to West Virginia to help coal miners form unions and fight for their rights.

Despite the strikes, coal companies made few changes. Many miners gave up hope and left the UMWA. In 1921, 42,000 miners belonged to the union, but by 1929 the number had dropped to only 1,000.

That same year marked the beginning of the Great Depression. Banks failed, businesses closed, and millions of workers lost their jobs. In West Virginia,

The U.S. government put many of West Virginia's jobless people back to work during the Great Depression. About 60,000 people built or repaired roads, many of which were in poor condition *(right)*.

The Great Depression was a hard time for many West Virginians.

the number of people without jobs was higher than in many other states.

To help West Virginia, the U.S. government created new jobs. Workers were hired to build roads and clear hiking paths through the state's forests.

New laws also improved working conditions. Workdays were shortened to eight hours. Companies had to pay workers a minimum wage, and they could no longer prevent their workers from joining unions. As a result, more West Virginian coal miners than ever before joined the UMWA.

During World War II, the world's largest synthetic rubber factory was built in Institute, West Virginia.

West Virginia's mines thrived during World War II (1939–1945), when coal was needed to fuel factory furnaces and freight trains. Workers in the state produced steel, ships, and weapons. Salt was used to manufacture plastic, rubber, and other products useful during wartime.

After the war, demand for coal dropped, as oil and natural gas became the nation's major sources of energy. At the same time, West Virginia's mines began to use machines that dug up more coal than miners could. Less coal and fewer mines were needed, and many workers lost their jobs. Thousands left the state in the 1950s and 1960s to look for work elsewhere.

To help the state's economy, the U.S. government created a program in 1965 to retrain workers in West Virginia and in other Appalachian states. Jobless coal miners learned the skills needed for building roads, for restoring forest-land, and for other occupations.

In the 1970s, a nationwide shortage of oil created a strong demand for West Virginia's coal. New mining jobs attracted people to the state. Jobs in the state's growing chemical, metal, and glass industries also helped West Virginia's population grow. By 1980 the Mountain State had more than 1.9 million residents.

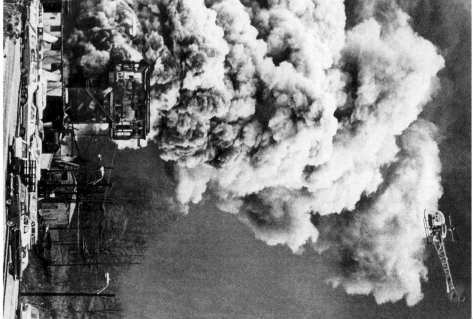

An explosion in 1968 at a West Virginian coal mine led to new safety laws.

One of West Virginia's most popular tourist attractions is The National Radio Astronomy Observatory in Green Bank. It is home to some of the largest radio telescopes in the world.

When the oil shortage ended in the 1980s, mines in West Virginia closed down, and coal miners again lost their jobs. By 1984 more people were out of work in West Virginia than anywhere else in the country. By 1990 West Virginia's population had dropped to 1.7 million residents.

West Virginians are looking for ways to make their economy less dependent on coal. By building better roads, the state has improved transportation. This has attracted some new industries, including tourism, to West Virginia. Thousands of workers earn a living helping tourists discover and enjoy the natural beauty and history of the Mountain State, a place West Virginians are proud to call home.

Several federal projects in the 1990s created new jobs for West Virginians, including jobs in highway construction and water development. In 2000 the number of people without jobs in West Virginia reached the lowest it has been since the state started keeping track in 1976. West Virginians have done many good things for their state and feel a lot of hope for the future.

A Growing Service State

cho and Falling Rock. Droop and Hominy Falls. Big Chimney and Tornado. About two-thirds of West Virginia's 1.8 million residents live in these and other small towns and rural areas across the state. Cities such as Charleston (the state capital), Huntington, Wheeling, Parkersburg, and Morgantown are home to the rest of the Mountain State's population.

Most Mountaineers—95 percent—trace their ancestry to immigrants from European countries such as Germany, Ireland, and Italy. African Americans make up about 3 percent of the population. Native Americans, Asian Americans, and Latinos together number less than 2 percent of the state's residents.

Cliff-hanging challenges abound for rock climbers in West Virginia.

West Virginia's landscape is dotted with small towns.

In the 1800s, most West Virginians made a living on a family farm. In 2000 only about 3 percent of all working West Virginians had jobs in agriculture. Most farms in the Mountain State are small and located in river valleys. Farmers raise beef and dairy cattle, chickens, and turkeys. West Virginia's crops include hay, corn, and tobacco. Apples and peaches are grown in the eastern part of the state.

Salt is still important to West Virginia's mining economy. But coal makes more money for the state than any other mineral. In fact, rich deposits of coal lie under half of West Virginia's land. About 4 per-cent of the state's workers have mining jobs. They

Some West Virginia tobacco farmers use mules to pull plows.

dig coal and pump natural gas and oil. Other miners scoop up sand for making glass and concrete. Limestone is crushed and used in building roads.

About 86,000 workers—or 10 percent of all jobholders in West Virginia—earn a living from manufacturing. Steel mills in the state use iron ore from the Midwest to make sheets of steel and giant beams for construction.

The state has become a leader in harvesting timber due to its abundant forests of oak, cherry, and other hardwood trees.

Other products are made from West Virginia's natural resources. Chemical plants along the Ohio and Kanawha Rivers use local supplies of salt, coal, natural gas, and oil to make dyes, paints, plastics, rubber, soaps, and other chemical products.

West Virginia is famous for its pottery and glass-ware. Workers at pottery plants mold clay into dishes, bricks, and tiles. Using local sand, the state's glassware factories turn out dinner glasses, bottles, stained glass, and large sheets of glass. Most workers in West Virginia have service jobs

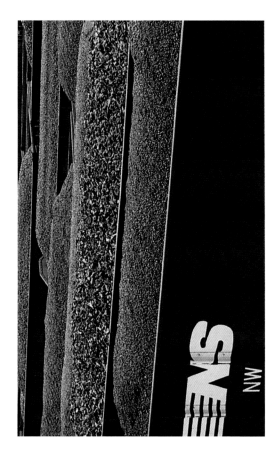

West Virginia produces more coal than all other states except Wyoming.

Some of the state's lumber is shipped to mills like this one to make paper.

helping people and businesses. Service workers include doctors, lawyers, and cooks. Even the hot dog vendors working at a Mountaineers football game at West Virginia University have service jobs.

The salesclerks who sell West Virginia's glassware and chemical products are also part of the service workforce. So are the people who load the Mountain State's coal and lumber onto barges and trains headed for market. Altogether, 60 percent of working West Virginians have service jobs.

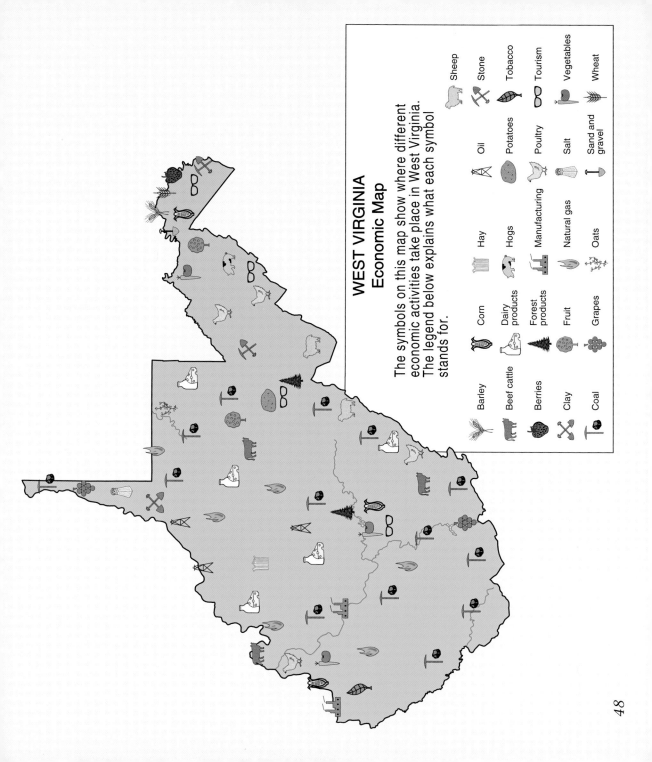

WEST VIRGINIA
Economic Map

The symbols on this map show where different economic activities take place in West Virginia. The legend below explains what each symbol stands for.

	Barley		Corn		Hay		Sheep
	Beef cattle		Dairy products		Hogs		Stone
	Berries		Forest products		Manufacturing		Tobacco
	Clay		Fruit		Natural gas		Tourism
	Coal		Grapes		Oats		Vegetables
					Oil		Wheat
					Potatoes	
					Poultry	
					Salt	
					Sand and gravel	

48

White-water rafting guides, who help rafters take on West Virginia's rapids, are among the state's many service workers.

Service workers also help the millions of tourists who come to West Virginia each year. Many visitors enjoy the thrill of rafting down the New and the Gauley Rivers, which are known for their white-water rapids. Cyclists tour the Greenbrier River Trail, an old railroad bed that passes through many small towns, over 35 bridges, and through two tunnels. Government workers, like firefighters and police officers, make up 17 percent of West Virginia's working people.

Campers head for West Virginia's many parks and forests, where they can also hike, ski, or ride horses and mountain bikes. Rock climbers can test their skills on the 900-foot cliff at Seneca Rocks. Each winter, ski resorts attract downhill skiers, who zoom down the state's snow-covered Appalachian peaks.

The people of the Appalachian Mountains are known for their unique culture. At the Augusta Heritage Center of Davis & Elkins College in Elkins, visitors can learn to play and sing traditional bluegrass tunes. Dancers can attend classes on Appalachian clogging, while other students discover how to weave baskets and sew quilts.

Each September in Clarksburg, the popular West Virginia Italian Heritage Festival offers lively entertainment by singers, dancers, and puppeteers dressed in colorful costumes. Actors recreate the first land battle of the Civil War for the Blue and Gray

West Virginia's countryside offers long, scenic roads that are perfect for bicycling.

Reunion during the first weekend of June in Philippi. Artillery demonstrations and a costumed Civil War ball are also part of the festivities.

Many people enjoy the Mountain State's music festivals. Every July thousands of people jam the streets of Wheeling on their way to hear famous country-music singers at Jamboree in the Hills. Mountaineers perform gospel tunes at the Vandalia Gathering in Charleston. And no trip to West Virginia is complete without tapping your toes at one of the state's many bluegrass festivals.

Large crowds gather for a country music festival in Wheeling.

West Virginia offers many opportunities to discover the state's history. Visitors to the Grave Creek Mound in Moundsville can learn about the mound-building Indians who once lived in the area. The pioneer cabin at Charleston's Cultural Center shows what daily life was like for the state's early settlers. A visit to the John Brown Museum in Harpers Ferry is a good way to learn about the events that led to the Civil War.

Visitors to West Virginia may choose to take a tour of a real coal mine.

At the Beckley Exhibition Coal Mine, groups go underground to see how miners dug for coal in the late 1800s. Those who prefer to travel back in time above the ground can learn more about West Virginia's history aboard the Cass Scenic Railroad. This old-fashioned steam-powered train takes passengers up the steep slopes of Bald Knob Mountain, the second highest point in the state. From here, viewers can look out over the rugged landscape and feel a bit of Mountaineer pride themselves.

Aboard the Cass Scenic Railroad, visitors can travel back in time and catch a view from the second highest point in the state.

Cleaning Up Solid Waste

In 1997 West Virginians threw out about 1.3 million tons of household trash and other garbage, also known as solid waste. That's about 3,500 tons of garbage every day, or more than 4 pounds per person per day.

More than 75 percent of West Virginia's garbage gets buried in **landfills**—giant pits dug in the earth for burying solid waste. In addition, some of the state's trash is dropped unlawfully on the side of the road and at thousands of other illegal dumps across the state.

Before the 1990s, along with its own waste, West Virginia routinely buried solid waste from nearby states, such as Pennsylvania, New York, and New Jersey. These states, which have high populations and overflowing landfills, paid West Virginia to dispose of extra garbage. In 1990, for example, West Virginia buried almost 750,000 tons of garbage from outside the Mountain State.

In the early 1990s, West Virginians realized that they would soon be over their heads in garbage if something did not change. The amount of out-of-state garbage was increasing, and lines of garbage trucks waiting to dump their loads at landfills were getting longer and longer. The number of garbage truck accidents and spills was also rising.

Landfills that were expected to fill up in 20 years were overflowing after only 7 years. There were no laws to limit the amount of garbage that could be buried in the state. As a result, West Virginia was quickly using up land and spending a lot of money to build new landfills.

This trash was left in a place that isn't meant for garbage.

To keep garbage under control, West Virginia passed a solid waste law in 1991. This law limits the amount of garbage that can be dumped at each landfill to 30,000 tons per month. West Virginia started programs to help clean up open dumps and scrap-tire piles. The state also created a new recycling program to help residents cut down on the amount of garbage going into landfills.

Through the recycling program, West Virginia's goal is to recycle 50 percent (based on the amount of garbage generated in the state in 1991) of its solid waste by the year 2010. By reducing the amount of garbage and increasing recycling, West Virginia is slowing down the rate at which landfills

People use bulldozers to pack trash in landfills.

Mountaineers concerned about garbage in their state put up signs to express their views.

fill up. The state has also increased jobs related to recycling.

West Virginians are participating in the plan to reduce garbage in many ways. Residents place glass, newspapers, plastics, and other recyclable materials at the curb for weekly or monthly pickup. Or they can take their recyclables to local recycling centers or solid waste authorities. Government offices have been buying and using recycled paper and other recycled products. Many of the state's newspaper publishers are using recycled newsprint in the newspapers. And West Virginia's schools are teaching students about solid waste and recycling. West Virginia also participates in America Recycles Day every November 15. This day helps promote recycling by educating the public about recycling and encouraging people to purchase recycled products.

Garbage Soup

The garbage placed in landfills eventually begins to decompose, or rot, turning into a soupy liquid called **leachate**. Rainwater filters down through the rotting trash and mixes with the leachate. This garbage soup, which carries germs and poisonous chemicals, soaks into the soil beneath the landfill and eventually pollutes the **groundwater**. This valuable source of drinking water for homes and businesses can then become unsafe to use.

To prevent leachate from reaching the groundwater, West Virginia requires workers to line new landfills with layers of heavy clay soil or thick plastic. Many landfills are also built with special drainage layers that collect the leachate, which is then piped to nearby sewage plants to be treated.

West Virginia no longer buries waste from other states. In fact, some garbage is being sent to be buried in bordering states such as Kentucky, Ohio, and Pennsylvania.

The efforts of individuals, businesses, and state and local agencies are paying off. West Virginia is burying less garbage and hopes to bury even less in the near future. West Virginians want to work together to make sure the Mountain State stays wild and wonderful.

As part of the state's Adopt-a-Highway Program, West Virginians pick up trash along roads and highways.

Many residents and visitors enjoy kayaking under the New River Gorge Bridge (*above*).

Fun Facts

The New River Gorge Bridge near Fayetteville, West Virginia, is the second highest bridge in the United States. The top of this steel arch bridge stands almost 900 feet above the New River.

Scientists from all over the world come to the National Radio Astronomy Observatory in Green Bank, West Virginia, to study outer space using the observatory's giant radio telescopes.

One of the nation's largest Native American burial grounds can be found in Moundsville. The mound is 900 feet around and 69 feet high.

The nation's first Mother's Day was celebrated in Grafton, West Virginia, on May 10, 1908. Just a few months later, on July 5, residents of Fairmont, West Virginia, marked the first Father's Day.

On January 26, 1960, Danny Heater of Burnsville, West Virginia, scored 135 points in a high school basketball game. His great shooting earned him a world record for the most points scored in a basketball game.

In 1912 farmers in central West Virginia became the first in the nation to raise Golden Delicious apples. Each fall the town of Clay, West Virginia, hosts the Golden Delicious Festival to celebrate this popular fruit.

Factories in Parkersburg, West Virginia, manufacture most of the glass marbles produced in the United States.

STATE SONG

"The West Virginia Hills" was adopted as one of three official state songs in 1963. The others are "This Is My West Virginia" and "West Virginia, My Home Sweet Home."

THE WEST VIRGINIA HILLS

Music by H. E. Engle; words by Ellen King

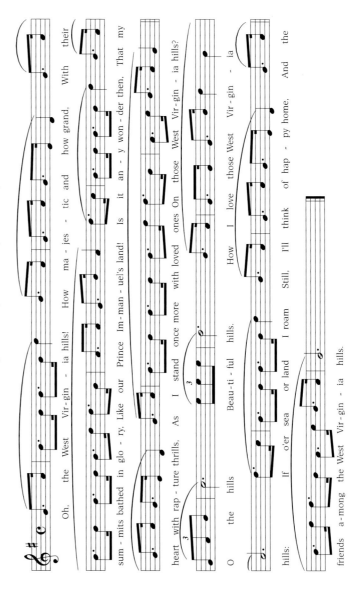

A WEST VIRGINIA RECIPE

Biscuits have been a staple of West Virginian meals since colonial times. Biscuits were especially popular in early America because they remained fresh for long periods of time. This biscuit recipe is both simple and delicious. Make sure an adult helps you with all steps using an oven.

CREAMY BISCUITS

2 cups plain flour
1 teaspoon salt
3 tablespoons unsalted butter
2½ teaspoons baking powder
2 tablespoons vegetable shortening
¾ cup cream

1. Have an adult preheat the oven to 450° F.
2. Sift flour, salt, and baking powder in large bowl.
3. Mix in butter and vegetable shortening until mixture has texture of crumbs.
4. Stir in cream to create soft dough.
5. Flour a bread board or other clean surface.
6. Roll dough on board until it's about ½ inch thick.
7. With 2½-inch biscuit cutter or drinking glass, divide into 2½-inch circles.
8. On ungreased baking sheet, bake for 10–15 minutes, or until golden brown.

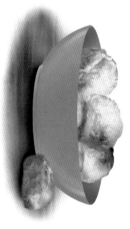

Makes about 9 biscuits.

HISTORICAL TIMELINE

13,000 B.C. Indian hunters first arrive in what later became West Virginia.

1000 B.C. Mound builders live along the Ohio River.

A.D. 1500 Mound builders abandon their villages.

1607 British settlers arrive in the Virginia Colony.

1671 Batts and Fallam claim the New River Valley for Great Britain.

1763 Great Britain wins the French and Indian War (1754–1763) and gains control of almost all the land between the Atlantic Ocean and the Mississippi River.

1775 British colonists in North America begin fighting to win their independence from Great Britain.

1783 Colonists defeat the British and form the United States of America.

1815 Factories in Charleston produce 3,000 bushels of salt daily.

1852 The Baltimore & Ohio Railroad lays tracks to Wheeling.

1859   John Brown raids Harpers Ferry.

1861   The Civil War (1861–1865) begins. Soldiers in western Virginia side with the North.

1863   West Virginia becomes the 35th state.

1900   Immigration swells West Virginia's population to almost 1 million.

1929   The Great Depression begins.

1958   Robert C. Byrd first wins election to the U.S. Senate, beginning a career that spans more than 40 years.

1968   An explosion at a coal mine in West Virginia leads to the creation of new safety laws.

1991   West Virginia passes a solid waste law to protect the state's groundwater.

2000   Unemployment in West Virginia reaches a record low.

OUTSTANDING WEST VIRGINIANS

George Brett (born 1953), a baseball player from Glen Dale, West Virginia, was named the American League's Most Valuable Player in 1980 for his high batting average. Brett retired in 1993 after 20 years with the Kansas City Royals. Brett became a member of the baseball Hall of Fame in 1999.

Bricktop (1894–1984) was an entertainer and nightclub owner whose nickname came from her flaming red hair and freckles. Born Ada Smith in Alderson, West Virginia, she moved to Paris and opened Bricktop's in the 1920s. The famous club featured American music and drew many well-known patrons.

Tony Brown (born 1933), a noted social leader, is the host of *Tony Brown's Journal*, a television program that has explored social issues from an African American perspective for more than 20 years. Raised in Charleston, Brown founded the Howard University School of Communications in Washington, D.C., in 1971 to help blacks succeed in the communications field.

Pearl S. Buck (1892–1973) drew upon her experiences growing up in China to become an award-winning author. In 1932 she received a Pulitzer Prize for her most famous book, *The Good Earth*. Born in Hillsboro, West Virginia, Buck was awarded the Nobel Prize for literature in 1938.

Robert C. Byrd (born 1917) broadcast weekly sermons on the radio and ran a grocery store before entering politics in the 1940s. Raised in the coal-mining town of Stotesbury, West Virginia, Byrd has served in the U.S. Senate since 1959.

George Brett

Tony Brown

Pearl S. Buck

Robert C. Byrd

Johnson Newlon Camden (1828–1908) was a businessman from Braxton County, West Virginia. He helped develop the oil industry in West Virginia in the 1860s. Later, he organized the Ohio River Railroad and was president of the West Virginia and Pittsburgh Railroad.

Phyllis Curtin (born 1927) first sang at the New York City Opera in 1959. A leading soprano, Curtin also sang at the Metropolitan Opera and performed with orchestras across the world. Curtin is from Clarksburg, West Virginia.

Joanne Dru (1923–1996) was a leading actress in many Western film classics, such as *Red River*, *Wagonmaster*, and *She Wore a Yellow Ribbon*. Dru was from Logan, West Virginia.

Thomas ("Stonewall") Jackson (1824–1863), born in Clarksburg, West Virginia, led Confederate troops to victory over Union forces in several major Civil War battles. The Confederate general earned his nickname because of the way he stood his ground "like a stone wall" at the First Battle of Bull Run in 1861.

Don Knotts (born 1924) is a comic actor known for his role as the deputy on *The Andy Griffith Show*, a popular television program of the 1960s. A native of Morgantown, West Virginia, Knotts also starred in television and movie comedies.

John Knowles (born 1926) is a writer from Fairmont, West Virginia. His first and best-known novel, *A Separate Peace*, was published in 1960. His later works include *Indian Summer* and *Peace Breaks Out*.

Stonewall Jackson

Joanne Dru

Phyllis Curtin

Johnson Camden

Gino Marchetti (born 1927), elected to the Pro Football Hall of Fame in 1972, was born in Smithers, West Virginia. A defensive end for the Baltimore Colts, Marchetti played in 11 straight Pro Bowls and was named All-Pro seven times before retiring in 1966.

Peter Marshall (born 1930) won five Emmy Awards as the host of *The Hollywood Squares.* Starting in 1966, he questioned famous guests in more than 5,000 editions of the tic-tac-toe television game show. The brother of Joanne Dru, Marshall was born in Huntington, West Virginia.

Peter Marshall

Kathy Mattea (born 1959) is a country music singer and songwriter who was born in Cross Lanes, West Virginia. Her first number-one country hits were "Goin' Gone" and "Eighteen Wheels and a Dozen Roses." She has won five Country Music Association Awards, four Academy of Country Music Awards, and two Grammys.

Kathy Mattea

Walter Dean Myers (born 1937), a native of Martinsburg, West Virginia, writes about the lives of young African Americans. Among his most famous children's books are *The Young Landlords* and *Motown and Didi: A Love Story,* both of which won a Coretta Scott King Award. His book *Somewhere in the Darkness* won a Newbery Honor Award in 1993.

Walter Dean Myers

Mary Lou Retton (born 1968) is a gymnast who gained fame at the 1984 Olympics as the first American to win a gold medal in the women's all-around gymnastics competition. Winning three additional medals, the native of Fairmont, West Virginia, earned more awards than any other U.S. athlete at that year's games.

Mary Lou Retton

Henry Ford Sinclair (1876–1953), born in Wheeling, West Virginia, founded the Sinclair Consolidated Oil Corporation in 1919 and built it into a multimillion-dollar business. The corporation operated gas stations across the country and owned millions of acres of oil fields in many parts of the world.

Cyrus Vance (born 1917), a lawyer and diplomat from Clarksburg, West Virginia, was appointed U.S. secretary of state under President Jimmy Carter. From 1991 to 1993, Vance served as a United Nations representative, working to resolve the conflict in Bosnia-Herzegovina (formerly part of Yugoslavia).

Booker T. Washington (1856–1915) was one of the most important black leaders and educators in the United States. He founded and became president of the Tuskegee Institute, a vocational school for black people in Tuskegee, Alabama. He advised presidents Theodore Roosevelt and William Howard Taft on racial issues and frequently toured the country giving speeches. His family moved to West Virginia when he was nine years old.

Jerry West (born 1938) grew up in Chelyan, West Virginia. A guard for basketball's Los Angeles Lakers, West retired in 1974 with the fourth-best career scoring average in the National Basketball Association's history. He was head coach of the Lakers from 1976 to 1979 and became general manager in 1982. He went on to become the Lakers' executive vice president until his retirement in 2000.

Bill Withers (born 1938), a singer and songwriter whose style combines funk, soul, and jazz, was born in Slab Fork, West Virginia. He has recorded several top hits, including "Ain't No Sunshine," "Lean on Me," and "Just the Two of Us"—a song that won a Grammy Award in 1982.

Cyrus Vance

Jerry West

Bill Withers

Henry Ford Sinclair

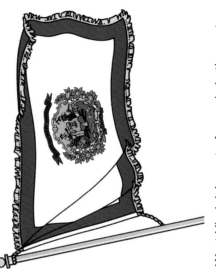

West Virginia's coat of arms is in the center of the state's flag. It displays a rock with the date West Virginia became a state. Beneath the date on a banner ribbon is West Virginia's motto—*Montani Semper Liberi* (Mountaineers Are Always Free).

FACTS-AT-A-GLANCE

Nickname: Mountain State

Songs: "The West Virginia Hills," "This Is My West Virginia," "West Virginia. My Home Sweet Home"

Motto: *Montani Semper Liberi* (Mountaineers Are Always Free)

Flower: rhododendron

Tree: sugar maple

Bird: cardinal

Animal: black bear

Fruit: Golden Delicious apple

Butterfly: monarch butterfly

Fish: brook trout

Date and ranking of statehood: June 20, 1863, the 35th state

Capital: Charleston

Area: 24,087 square miles

Rank in area, nationwide: 41st

Average January temperature: 32° F

Average July temperature: 72° F

POPULATION GROWTH

Millions

This chart shows how West Virginia's population has grown from 1800 to 2000.

West Virginia's seal shows a miner and a farmer with two rifles in front of them. A banner above them reads "State of West Virginia," while below is the state motto.

Population: 1,808,344 (2000 census)

Rank in population, nationwide: 37th

Major cities and populations: (2000 census)
Charleston (53,421), Huntington (51,475), Parkersburg (33,099), Wheeling (31,419), Morgantown (26,809)

U.S. senators: 2

U.S. representatives: 3

Electoral votes: 5

Natural resources: brine, clay, coal, crushed stone, fertile soil, limestone, natural gas, oil, petroleum, rock salt, sand and gravel, sandstone, shale

Agricultural products: apples, beef cattle, chickens, corn, hay, milk, peaches, tobacco, turkeys

Manufactured goods: baked goods, detergents, dyes, glassware, mining machinery, nickel, paints, pipes, plastics, pottery, salt cake, sheet and structural steel, soft drinks, synthetic rubber, tin plate, tools

WHERE WEST VIRGINIANS WORK

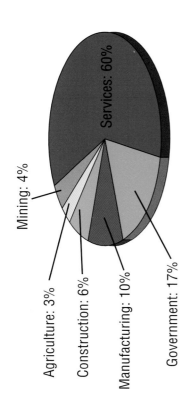

Services—60 percent
(services includes jobs in trade; community, social, and personal services; finance, insurance, and real estate; transportation, communication, and utilities)

Government—17 percent

Manufacturing—10 percent

Construction—6 percent

Mining—4 percent

Agriculture—3 percent

GROSS STATE PRODUCT

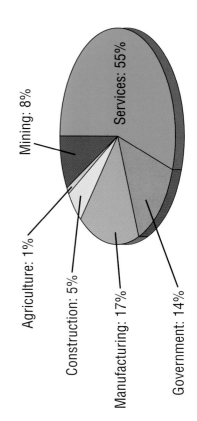

Services—55 percent

Manufacturing—17 percent

Government—14 percent

Mining—8 percent

Construction—5 percent

Agriculture—1 percent

WEST VIRGINIA WILDLIFE

Mammals: black bear, fox, mink, opossum, raccoon, white-tailed deer

Birds: bald eagle, croppie, flycatcher, hawk, kingfisher, owl, sauger, thrush, warbler

Amphibians and reptiles: lizards, snakes, turtles

Fish: bass, catfish, trout, walleyed pike

Trees: beech, cherry, hemlock, hickory, maple, oak, poplar, red spruce, white pine

Wild plants: aster, azalea, bloodroot, goldenrod, hepatica, rhododendron

Owls are one of many types of birds found in West Virginia.

PLACES TO VISIT

Beckley Exhibition Coal Mine, Beckley

Visitors can go 1,500 feet underground into a former working coal mine. Guided by former miners, visitors tour the mine in remodeled mine cars. Original camp houses and a mining museum are nearby.

Blackwater Falls State Park, Davis

This lovely park contains a wooded canyon in which the Blackwater River drops 65 feet. Visitors can picnic, ride bicycles, hike, enjoy nature programs, and do other outdoor activities.

Cass Scenic Railroad, Cass

Visitors can take a scenic steam-train tour that departs from the tiny old railroad logging town of Cass. Riders go through stunning mountain scenery to the top of Bald Knob, to Whitaker Station, or to Spruce.

Harpers Ferry National Historical Park

Several important events took place on this site, including the 1859 slave uprising led by John Brown. The streets of the historic town have been fully restored. Visitors learn about John Brown, the Civil War, African American history, and much more.

Huntington Museum of Art, Huntington

West Virginia's largest museum is known for its collection of English, French, and American paintings, as well as historical glass. The museum is perched on a hilltop, and its grounds feature nature trails, a sculpture garden, and a plant conservatory.

Lost World Caverns, Lewisburg

These enormous caverns contain rooms that measure about 1,000 feet by 75 feet. The caverns also feature waterfalls, stalagmites, and stone formations.

National Radio Astronomy Observatory, Green Bank

Built in a mountain valley, the observatory houses many telescopes, including a giant 140-foot telescope. The facility has guided tours, exhibits, an audiovisual show, and demonstrations of equipment.

Pearl S. Buck Birthplace Museum, Hillsboro

Buck, the first American woman to win both a Pulitzer Prize and a Nobel Prize for literature, was born on this site in 1892. The white frame house was restored in 1958 and sits in the hills of the Appalachian Mountains. Inside, visitors can see original furnishings and Buck memorabilia.

Seneca Rocks, Riverton

Rock climbers enjoy scaling these cliffs. Hikers can take a trail that leads to a spectacular view at the top of the 900-foot cliffs.

South Charleston Mound, South Charleston

Mound builders built this nearly 2,000-year-old mound as a burial site for chieftains. It measures 175 feet across and 35 feet high.

ANNUAL EVENTS

Appalachian Heritage Weekend, Pipestem—*March*

Feast of the Ramson, Richwood—*April*

Blue and Gray Reunion, Philippi—*June*

Mountain State Arts and Crafts Fair, Ripley—*July*

West Virginia State Fair, Lewisburg—*August*

Civil War Days, Carnifex Ferry Battlefield State Park—*September*

Country Roads Festival, Ansted—*September*

West Virginia Oil and Gas Festival, Sistersville—*September*

Mountain State Forest Festival, Elkins—*October*

Old Tyme Christmas, Harpers Ferry—*December*

LEARN MORE ABOUT WEST VIRGINIA

BOOKS

General

Fazio, Wende. *West Virginia*. Danbury, CT: Children's Press, 2000. For older readers.

Fradin, Dennis B. and Judith Bloom Fradin. *West Virginia*. Chicago: Children's Press, 1996.

Special Interest

Anderson, Joan. *Pioneer Children of Appalachia*. New York: Houghton Mifflin, 1990. A portrait of what life was like for the early pioneers of Appalachia. Text and photographs bring readers back to the early 1800s by showing the daily life of the fictional Davis family at a living-history museum near Salem, West Virginia.

Brett, George. *George Brett: From Here to Cooperstown*. Lenexa, KS: Addax Publishing Group, 1999. This lively look at the National Baseball Hall of Famer's career includes photographs of games, letters, contracts, uniforms, bats, and other memorabilia. For older readers.

Fritz, Jean. *Stonewall*. New York: Putnam Publishing Group, 1997. This brief, informative biography shares the life of Thomas "Stonewall" Jackson, a Southern general from West Virginia who played a major role in the Civil War.

Streissguth, Tom. *John Brown*. Minneapolis, MN: Carolrhoda Books, Inc., 1999. This biography of John Brown tells about his upbringing and his fight against slavery. It also describes the slave uprising Brown led at Harpers Ferry in 1859.

Fiction

Belton, Sandra. *McKendree*. New York: Greenwillow Books, 2000. This is the story of Tilara Haynes, a young girl living in West Virginia who finds out a bit about love, herself, and life while spending time at a home for the elderly called McKendree.

Naylor, Phyllis Reynolds. *Shiloh*. New York: Atheneum, 1991. Eleven-year-old Marty Preston loves to spend time in the hills behind his home near Friendly, West Virginia. In this Newbery Award–winning book, Marty learns how hard it can be to separate right from wrong when he struggles to save a dog, Shiloh, from being mistreated by its cruel owner.

WEBSITES

State of West Virginia

<http: //www.state.wv.us>

West Virginia's official home page includes government news and facts about state services and provides links to community activities.

West Virginia's Official Visitor Website

<http://www.westvirginia.com>

West Virginia's tourism website provides up-to-date information on traveling around the state, camping, whitewater rafting, and a calendar of events.

The Charleston Gazette

<http://www.wvgazette.com>

Read about current events in the online version of this popular West Virginia newspaper.

West Virginia Legislature

<http://www.legis.state.wv.us/>

This site includes a daily summary of activity in West Virginia's legislature, as well as a kids' page.

PRONUNCIATION GUIDE

Allegheny (al-uh-GAY-nee)

Appalachian (ap-uh-LAY-chuhn)

Cherokee (CHEHR-uh-kee)

Greenbrier (GREEN-bry-ur)

Iroquois (IHR-uh-kwoy)

Kanawha (kuh-NAW-wuh)

Mingo (MIHNG-goh)

Monongahela (muh-nahn-guh-HEE-luh)

Potomac (puh-TOH-mihk)

Seneca (SEHN-ih-kuh)

Shawnee (shaw-NEE)

Monongahela National Forest

GLOSSARY

colony: a territory ruled by a country some distance away

constitution: the system of basic laws or rules of a government, society, or organization; the document in which these laws or rules are written

groundwater: water that lies beneath the earth's surface. The water comes from rain and snow that seep through soil into the cracks and other openings in rocks. Groundwater supplies wells and springs.

immigrant: a person who moves into a foreign country and settles there

landfill: a place specially prepared for burying solid waste

leachate: liquid that has seeped through waste or that forms when waste rots in a landfill. Leachate can contaminate water or soil.

plantation: a large estate, usually in a warm climate, on which crops are grown by workers who live on the estate. In the past, plantation owners usually used slave labor.

plateau: a large, relatively flat area that stands above the surrounding land

precipitation: rain, snow, and other forms of moisture that fall to earth

treaty: an agreement between two or more groups, usually having to do with peace or trade

INDEX

PHOTO ACKNOWLEDGMENTS

Cover photographs by © Ron Watts/CORBIS. © Kit Kittle/CORBIS; PresentationMaps.com, pp. 1, 8, 9, 48; © Richard T. Nowitz/ CORBIS, pp. 2–3, 3, 12; © Richard Cummins/CORBIS, (detail) 4, (detail) 7, (detail) 17, (detail) 42, (detail) 54; Jerry Hennen, pp. 6, 11, 13, 44; David Dvorak, Jr., pp. 6 (inset), 15 (right); IPS, p. 10, 66 (bottom), 69 (second from top); © Scott T. Smith, pp. 14, 40, 46; © Conrad A. Gutra/Root Resources, p. 15 (left); © 1995 Charles Braswell, Jr., p. 16: Smithsonian Institution, #80-1819, p. 18; Stephen J. Shaluta, Jr., pp. 19, 42, 50; Bettmann/ COR-BIS, pp. 20, 32; The Library of Virginia, pp. 21, 24 (left), 28; West Virginia State Archives, pp. 22, 23, 31, 35, 67 (top), 68 (bottom); Dictionary of American Portraits, p. 24 (right); Library of Congress, pp. 25, 27, 29, 33, 37, 38; Washington/Custis/Lee Collection, Washington and Lee University, Lexington, Virginia, p. 26; WV & Regional History Collection, WV University Library, p. 34; Alexandria Library, Lloyd House, p. 36; Lawrence Pierce, *Charleston Gazette*, p. 39; © 1995 Thomas R. Fletcher, p. 43; © W. Lynn Seldon, Jr., pp. 45, 55; © Tim Wright/CORBIS, p. 47; Barbara L. Moore/NE Stock Photo, p. 49; Larry Belcher, p. 51; © 1994 Pat Wadecki/Root Resources, p. 52; © Kenneth Layman/Photo Agora, p. 53; WV Solid Waste Management Board, p. 56; Jim West/Impact Visuals, p. 57; © 2001 Jay Mallin, p. 58; WV Division of Natural Resources, p. 59; Frederica Georgia, p. 60; Jack Lindstrom, p. 61; Tim Seeley, pp. 63, 71, 72; Kansas City Royals, p. 66 (top); Tony Brown Productions, Inc., p. 66 (second from top); Pearl S. Buck, p. 66 (second from bottom); Metropolitan Opera Archives, p. 67 (second from top); Hollywood Book & Poster, Co., p. 67 (second from bottom); U.S. Signal Corps, National Archives, p. 67 (bottom); Photofest, pp. 68 (top), 68 (second from top), 69 (bottom); Ken Petretti, p. 68 (second from bottom); American Heritage Center, University of Wyoming, p. 69 (top); Los Angeles Lakers, p. 69 (second from bottom); Jean Matheny, p. 70 (top); © 1992 Lydia Parker, p. 73; © Mary A. Root/Root Resources, p. 80.